Embracing
What We
Tell Ourselves

Embracing What We Tell Ourselves

EMMANUEL AGNANT

Charleston, SC
www.PalmettoPublishing.com

Embracing What We Tell Ourselves

First Edition

Hardcover ISBN: 979-8-8229-2372-0
Paperback ISBN: 979-8-8229-3175-6
eBook ISBN: 979-8-8229-3176-3

I would like to express my gratitude to everyone who has inspired me to write this, as well as to my wife for teaching me how to accept and improve upon my inner dialogue and for supporting my personal growth.

Reading built my focus and exposed my mind to a new world of imagination and ideas, while ultimately making me a better learner.

Writing allowed me to share my thoughts and experiences with the world.

I tell my friends that writing is not always easy, but it is always worth the effort of sharing my innermost thoughts and feelings.

Contents

Thursdays

Thursday marks the start of this, with its significance being its essence rather than its location. It is similar to a radiant star shining brightly in the universe of existence. Grammar isn't here—expressly reserved. Having everything in its proper place is important, even when we're feeling tired. Our surroundings, whatever they may be, can impact us greatly. The simple act of waking up is a gift that should not be taken for granted, and I hope you appreciate the game you're engaging in. Allow me to express this idea—consider how we all bear some kind of resemblance to others, and if you pay attention and avoid certain situations, you may be surprised by what you find. Whether it be a physical similarity, a shared interest or experience, or simply a common outlook on life, the connections we can make with others are endless and often unexpected. By keeping an open mind and taking the time to get to know those around us, we can discover a world of fascinating and meaningful relationships that we may have never known existed. So, the next time you find yourself in a new environment, take a moment to look for the similarities rather than the differences, and see what kind of connections you can make. It's similar to having an object or creature that is moving and then discovering that it's actually circuits. What steps should we take to retrieve it, and what is the desired outcome? Should we proceed with answering these questions? Sometimes I hear the southern accents needing me to get up to take a flight and then never save the date to go, days to complete, and times to stop. I'm sure you show up to a point where you want to opt out because freedom from activities will allow you to have some much-needed rest and relaxation. Shall we discuss ways to enjoy ourselves? Even while paying bills, I am determined to find joy. It seems like everyone talks about being unproductive. Perhaps creating a calendar for important events could help us start planning more enjoyable activities. As you enter your car and begin your journey, envision those who accompany you as a large group of supporters, perhaps even with celebratory music. We often boast of how effortlessly we skip Sunday services and arrive promptly to meetings, regardless of their duration. Some of this work has been done by captains, and it is difficult for me to give permission for them to stop thinking because I am unsure if anyone prepares the provisions in that manner. What about that bridge? I've been informed it's a brief stroll, and I opted to take a chance and disregard my doctor's advice, getting rid of habits through patches, laying the pullout for you to lay on, but it's temporary. I don't have any paper, and I can't stand doing things on a bad day. We will see if we can go ahead and start embracing what we tell ourselves.

I've always aspired to achieve something remarkable such as bringing up the challenge of the elusive sunshine, although it remains a difficult feat. Nonetheless, my intentions are sincere. It's always a promise that keeps a fire going, relying on someone else's acknowledgment to take a moment to breathe. Having to worry about the loop matter—let's be sure about this. Then you have to check if you're all right. Although I may not be thrilled, we have yet to respond to the door while accepting our self-talk. However, I have faith that you will know just the right words to say. Who will be under perception, at what times, and who will be accompanying the entire ship because you were offered to drive down Eisenhower? There are many tasks to accomplish, but I truly believe this opportunity is invaluable, knowing you watch that little place up there. I go to a small stretch of the highway and perform music as if I were on stage at a concert, calling it "the shadow by the body of water." Get ready to witness a week full of diligent work, delightful customer interactions, and an exhilarating atmosphere fueled by the beats of Dr. Dre "Nuthin' but a 'G' Thang", with Snoop Dogg. Hpnotiq drink is the ideal alcoholic beverage for me as it helps me worry less and stay more engaged in life. Additionally, meditation helps me cultivate a sense of gratitude for what I currently have, which in turn reduces my desire for material possessions and helps me recognize the abundance already present in my life. This perspective shift allows me to approach the idea of owning a house with a more level-headed and realistic mindset, rather than a frantic and anxious one. Overall, meditation supports my mental and emotional well-being, allowing me to approach life's decisions with greater ease, clarity, and peace. In any case, I went on to collect and tidy up my space, I couldn't help but feel a sense of accomplishment and clarity in my mind. However, I made my way back to the restroom once more. We don't have any graduation-related assignments to complete. Is graduation already here? Well, that means there's still a chance. I'm eager to participate in the ceremony and ask others, "Are you maintaining good progress?" And there is tough stuff; we can get through the tough stuff because of the pronunciations you know we have. Sometimes I wash my hair, but I always make sure to do it in the bathroom, whether we're hiking or purifying and cleansing. After completing the assignment, while still in class, do you know what happened? We are interesting characters. We go around the interesting things and go about our business, thinking about the words that we write. "Who is this guy?" Bet he has something important to say. People must be asking themselves. At certain levels of writing, a standard expectation is for the piece to contain ten thousand words, but you know what? It does add up. Check out the transfer offers and ascertain their pricing before perhaps proceeding after dinner. What do you consider the luckiest day of our lives? Are you kidding? I guess you do have a point. I'm still out there, so you're still out there. Are you updated and UV protected by Omi ancestors? Good, because if so, did you discover a face to the name yet? And you'll put it together, but it's a great bowl in a pouch. Think about some sprays that work within thirty minutes; however, there is one situation where you simply have to rise and move forward, as the revolution brings pain and turmoil leads to the breakdown of things.

The way you achieve unparalleled protection is demonstrated by your method of ironing out all the wrinkles and then moving forward with youthful enthusiasm. I will be attentive while you explain. There are times when you try to resist listening, but then you retreat to your home. However, it's acceptable since today is still Thursday. And Chairman, is there something you truly wish to discover? I am not 102 years old, but I am a weight-level-turnover-that-bounces-back-in-enough-to-go-on-my-way type of person, and people have nobody's numbers nowadays. Sometimes the risk is very rewarding, but right now you sometimes take a coffee cup out to the kitchen, sitting down and embracing what you tell yourself. Sometimes people react for favors; it's OK, you figure. I'm trying to sit there and not say a word, and then there's no date to push it or the time, but you gotta drive quick instructions. Do you perform any cleaning tasks after we close the door, or do you simply make calls and leave? Can you show me jobs that involve such minimal effort? I need you to wait for me another minute or two before doing what you intend. Hopefully you'll achieve your desired outcome. Conversations regarding music, books, history, and the withdrawn souls occasionally arise, and you enthusiastically engage in topics that interest you; yet even afterward, you find that your enthusiasm persists to an extent that lingers. Don't be discouraged; come on—a few more whatever attitudes get sent back to the committee. And then you spend time for one minute with yourself, and you understand it.

Who are the scientific remedy centers to dictate when you're feeling well or not? It's up to you to speak up or remain silent. I see that you helped a lot of people with such medicine, but if it's an open wound, how do we know? You used it for many years and haven't had a capillary attitude. Should I become fat if the milk is impure? We adhere to certain procedures and acknowledge that life entails setbacks, which can be very unsettling. It is a common occurrence. As previously mentioned, we cannot guarantee, but we will consult records and possibly seek the input of others, being very professional and diligent, not questioning our judgment; sometimes we get proven wrong. Having a drink of water before your lunch is important. It is challenging to confirm whether a medication has been prescribed in clinics, and it is equally difficult to give a straightforward answer. The prescription and its interpretation depend on the individual's understanding and interpretation. We need a sense of quietness while walking through nearby parks, bringing along a guidebook app to help me identify different plant and animal species and maybe even trying to spot some rare ones. It will give us a chance to unwind and recharge while still engaging our minds and senses. But if your plan is that you pay damages, what happens then? Imagine a situation where you are leisurely watching the gavel, but it's important for you to understand it because that's precisely why we opted for it. You need to ascend the house and take a look at that roof. You must find a way to accomplish it. You still gotta find a way to try to get a no-brainer refinance, so you get better protection—15 percent or 20 percent. It's something you definitely don't wanna miss out on. After receiving my response, you proceeded to apply for credit cards and were approved for a significant amount of money, which was added to your available credit. You then began receiving text message alerts for monitoring purposes, causing you to forget about managing your weight. Do you require any measurements or a temperature check? While walking and practicing control over your body, you are able to observe patterns and notifications, followed by receiving reliable traits that you can approve of.

While falling asleep, I contemplate whether I need to pay for something, but the thought of having to extract funds from my finances for additional expenses discourages me. Despite this uncertainty, I acknowledge the importance of being prepared for unforeseeable circumstances, even if it means sacrificing a certain evening. However, the possibility of the situation occurring leaves me unsure and ultimately dissuades me from pursuing the idea. Who you are is what I am, and nobody can take that away from us; they can't take that away from the good mornings, the good afternoons, and the good nights. We have been considering all the divisions, and we get more percentage out of the slowness of business. Are you sure you don't want to sell? But we ask ourselves in a minute, "What happens if we can't buy?" We always do the work, and then it's best to split it fifty-fifty.

Hold on; "Where do you think you're going?" I just want to catch up—can't keep waiting. Also I keep *no* money on me while walking around in a box. We take a swim for a minute, and let's say that some checks bring risk. Although it may seem more capable, we should remain authentic to our own abilities. Additionally let's discuss strategies to generate a $200 million income, even from our $200 pockets. Is there any progress? How would you feel if I told you that you have an invitation? What if I said you were attending a gathering where people commonly analyze others, and contemplating the effectiveness of such assessment in improving the world yields no positive outcome? It simply amounts to nothing. Softening your positions does not indicate weakness on your part. Observe how individuals are attracted to your affectionate vibe. Would you be interested in me accompanying you to the smoke shop to purchase various edibles? We can then go out for dinner and reminisce. You realize that being appointed and having appointments, people cancel. Although we are ordinary individuals present in this realm, we believe that individuals cannot be easily substituted since their exceptional perspectives and experiences are irreplaceable. Is it difficult to determine whether a particular moment is successful or disastrous? And even if we discuss it, can we adequately express our opinions? I am going to Bagel King, grabbing a sesame medium-toasted bagel, and asking for extra cream cheese and a cup of hot coffee to go with it. Well, we still have a few minutes. Since we have some time left and are financially stable, let's try to envision going camping without any possessions. I have to depart now as I am going to be exhausted and have plans to wrap up. Goodbye. And if we buy next Sunday, we'll also think about what we don't know yet about that deal. Then there's a luncheon going on Friday. Initially we consider the unpleasant experiences that lawyers may have to endure.

We might obtain art museum tickets, but that's not the main discussion. I intend to present items that can be covered in thirty minutes and highlight the advantages of contributing, which could generate media coverage. Can you consider responding and observe how we handle the situation when there's an elephant in the room? I have several important notes and alarms set for 10:47 a.m. Is this directed toward you? We usually discuss *Babylon* on Thursdays, but today we want to catch up with family and enjoy drinks on the brick porch wall, that had faded to a pale red. What do you want to have this time around? But maybe tomorrow or tonight, we'll talk about making changes and what time will be required. We have quiet manners in all quiet spaces. In all silent areas, we maintain a composed demeanor. We are undoubtedly aware and have burned off ten calories. How do you indicate dialogue? There's no chance that we are aware of the jacket's location—maybe it's in the SouthernEaze. The glass in the door shattered as a result of my breaking and smashing it into countless pieces. My intention was not to repeat this destructive behavior, and I have learned from my actions. There is no need to continue breaking the glass door. Occasionally individuals assert that our demeanor and our preference for a modest way of life conform to conventional expectations. But all I want to know about are the pieces of shattered glass and then move on to the next.

It's currently six o'clock and my body doesn't seem to be cooperating. I'm tired and doze off at the traffic signals. And we're already passing Beardsley State Park. I need to be back by tomorrow morning, so I'm grabbing the Red, White and Blueberry Pop-Tart from the toaster since the first one was cold. There's no need to engage in hostile arguments. The strongman leaves repeatedly. Along with a notary public and a woman who has an affinity for glass jars, we go about our nights. So if your car needs West End Auto Repair's work, you can drop it off. Are you avoiding intolerable contacts by going through doors and evading income tax? Who authored the phrase "I don't want to witness your departure in front of me." Ms. M. Quitman, please enlighten me on what else is required in finance, as I discovered that it demands departmental work, constant meetings, and a patient temperament. Are there individuals within the group who consistently perform well, handle situations efficiently, and don't encounter many issues? The European publication expressed appreciation toward me, and you are putting forth a great deal of effort. I no longer exhibit the same negative demeanor as before. After becoming a shining star, I will inspect photographic reminiscences and offer my services for $400. The article was prominently featured, but where is the monkey? It's time we reach out to many individuals about this matter. I'm not willing to contribute financially, so don't worry. You can use FaceTime to contact the others who have reached out to me. Perhaps it would be a good idea to have new plumbing installed for a more modern system. Additionally it should be announced over the loudspeaker that passport prices have increased this year. Lastly, for the tournaments, please add an extra shot of espresso with two sugars and a splash of cream. I'm hoping all goes well, like pioneers rolling backwoods blunt. The checking account has limited funds, yet they are requesting a thousand dollars for the small dog seen barking at the window. It appears to be a case of wealthy family perks. If you're not pronouncing things like that, it is what it is. I want to convey that I appreciate your presence, even if it's just a small amount, and that whenever I am in your company, I feel compelled to bid farewell. While I have considered finding a new job, resigning, or limiting my interactions, I have decided to continue my current dynamic. I'm unsure if I should fulfill my duty by choosing between going to China, Australia or south-east Tahiti. Instead of sticking to traditional work, I plan to leave a lasting impression by being myself—genuine and straightforward. I hope to be memorable, express myself well, and land interviews effortlessly, just like photos and videos. While still embracing what I tell myself, I come in on reading and writing books, putting stories out there for people. My ultimate goal is to have a single store that will serve as my official and permanent entry point. This may also be my final official act. Although we are not obliged to pursue fame, we tend to do so. However, I was advised to disregard all of that.

Yeah, we all know happy birthdays. I never know if you ever do anything special on it, and of course, I'm trying. Tomorrow I plan to head to the East to retrieve payment, but I can never anticipate the unforeseeable events that may occur. Perhaps you'll be interested in hearing about my dream regarding the world. How are you going to get to the hospital? Here is one of your appointment schedules: wait for organic lunch to come out here. I'll be afraid of a mile after tomorrow. I want to get out of here tonight and not at ten o'clock! We have enough other people, and again, we never know if they will make it in time.

Reporting a good story about human experiences is not sufficient if it ends up in the hands of the wrong recipient. Prioritize self-love before identifying with your family name for a complete sense of identity. I navigate various realms, discussing figures, grand residences, and current events. I feel that this is appropriate for my persona, as I am pursuing opportunities to speak on podcast channels. How many individuals are listening to my vocal expression? Are you still reachable via phone? What time is deemed enjoyable? Would it be feasible for me to venture out and live my life? She is not a melody nor is she someone who will arrive early. She possesses access to the automobile. It just dawned on me now that I'm going to do well. We need to get it immediately, which I'm gonna have to do. Could you add some peppers to it? Would it be overwhelming for you? Are you able to converse? And would it be too much trouble for you and then move on? There is nothing more important than getting a restful night's sleep and not overthinking.

I left a quarter past twelve, feeling unwell, and had a glass of water. By any chance do you possess vitamin C? Discreetly walking around, the name is being whispered. Do not deceive yourself. Next time try MoneyGram—just ring and come in. Being here and having to just stop, I understand coming back is like going away altogether. We have until four o'clock to raise enough money before leaving for Boston. Otherwise, we won't have enough funds for the trip. A week passed, we didn't actively work on it, but we remained calm, knowing that we always do things correctly and will receive acknowledgment for it throughout our lives. Spending thirty minutes can feel like a very long time when encountering challenges. However, I still have enough time to travel back to Connecticut. What is necessary? Let's have some enjoyment and play games without worrying about it. Just remember to maintain a healthy body. Please answer: "What does the phrase 'on the floor' signify to you?" The phone keeps ringing incessantly, with occasional sudden outbursts. Moreover, the middle of the night is as serene and captivating as ever. We are having a great time, blissfully asleep. Suddenly darkness prevails again, and we have been traveling in the car, side by side, for an extended period, like the day of the dead. The world has reached a mutual agreement, and the years of infancy are long gone. We laugh to avoid complications, as I recall a woman who has blueberry eyes and who should be cautious of the urge to have another drink. This is only the start as we travel for about a week, seeking profitable opportunities to acquire and later sell. I will be traveling to several states soon and am currently en route to the golf driving range that only accepts cash. For those of you who are in Texas and are planning on visiting Kansas and Colorado, have you thought about returning to the East? A shout-out to you. Despite this suggestion, your internal voice may object to every option. I inquired about the severity of the situation, not the outcome. The verdict will be revealed tomorrow, and if you're curious, you can call for more information. Try to prepare yourself emotionally but keep in mind that we have potential solutions to improve the situation. Let's begin by focusing on areas where there is a clear path forward. All of a sudden, as you're walking, you feel a sharp pain in the side of your body. And then you close the door and call for help, but your voice is south of a millionaire quiet. Time to start reminiscing about things in the actual world, not just in our digital lives.

We stuffed so many bell peppers that now we have nothing else. Then, as we sit in the back, I try to create conversation by bringing up unimportant topics. However, in reality, these topics are not useful. This leads to wasted reactions and a feeling of missing our true selves. As soon as you write your name on a flat piece of paper, we'll retrieve it from the valley and open it later. Since nobody wants to be here, I'll gladly embrace nature and make myself available to assist you with whatever you require at this moment. First, I'll get a cup and contemplate the music being produced. Afterward, we can pack it in the car and prepare some meals. We'll open the trunk once we arrive at the destination and assess where to place the tables. We'll chop it up in the kitchen right here. We are positive the food will be outstanding and plan to establish a nonprofit to provide three hundred meals daily. We will meet up with you soon. We have all the necessary vehicles and licenses. However, I struggle with social interactions as I am unsure of what people expect from me and often respond inappropriately. As a result I could potentially end up being isolated from the community for some time. Gradually we develop a desire to take action and effect change, and it is likely achievable. In present times, teaching lessons is challenging, thus leading by example becomes crucial. Consider life as a game, where you need not rush but rather start slowly and build a strong foundation. Relax and drift off to sleep with a pillow on your armrest after leaning toward the left. Having VIP access to any place is desirable. It's critical to have someone in life, as the one with money is busy catching lionfish. As we flip through the pages and reminisce, it's important to acknowledge that happiness is a choice, but it's admirable when someone actually attains it. We were naive to think that we could ignore our mistakes and move on, and now we must face the fact that we will never have the proper mindset or understanding. Despite this, we must still make the effort to stay in touch and feign interest in each other's lives. Although it is tempting to leave, there is still beauty to be found in our conversations if we take the time to appreciate it. This is a general statement not intended for anyone specific.

As we wait for freelance projects, our unique styles bring excitement to the table, and we take on party bookings despite the unpredictable outcome. Our work inspires us, and we take pride in it without any resistance. Time management is crucial, and we always deliver on time. However, sometimes our efforts don't get approved, and we have to accept rejection. We will vanish once we have everything gathered, and I am unaware of the whereabouts of your previous phones. Phones make constant noises during mealtimes, either from job offers or multiple part-time jobs to make ends meet, before returning to Fulton Street station. Preserve this moment, where you will have enough room to breathe. Afterward you will always possess what is needed. While it may be true that people often focus more on the negative aspects of things, such as routine vehicle maintenance, there are valid reasons for this behavior. In the case of vehicle maintenance, it is important to prioritize and address potential issues before they escalate. By maintaining our vehicles regularly, we can prevent breakdowns, ensure safety, and extend their lifespan, which ultimately saves us time, money, and hassle. Moreover, the environment can indeed become harsh if proper maintenance is neglected. Failing to replace worn-out tires or check the brakes can lead to accidents that harm people and the environment. By focusing on routine maintenance, we can reduce emissions, ensure fuel efficiency, and minimize our carbon footprint. Although discussions of routine vehicle maintenance may initially seem negative, they are essential reminders to take proactive measures in caring for our vehicles and the environment. It is important to approach these discussions with a positive mindset, recognizing the benefits of regular maintenance rather than solely focusing on the negatives. As we return to our starting point in Fox Creek, we are reminded of the rattles and noises we heard at Waters Ranch. However, our intention is not to compete with others but rather to pursue what brings us joy, while ensuring that we are not invading others' spaces. As the music builds up, we start moving our bodies in synchronization with the beats, spinning and twirling, lost in the rhythm of the music. The strange things around us seem to fade away as we get lost in the moment, our bodies moving effortlessly to the music. I can feel the sweat trickling down my back, but I keep dancing, not wanting to break the spell of the moment. The music slowly comes to an end, and we break out of our dance trance, laughing and smiling at each other. I take a deep breath, feeling energized and alive, grateful for this moment of escape from the strange things around us. Seeing our future visions is a pleasant experience that motivates us to explore what lies ahead in the spaces we may not have noticed before, especially after hearing the sound of birds flapping their wings and twigs snapping on the ground. The trunk is producing sounds, and whoever claims it will receive some items. These days, it arrives rapidly, and we hear music before scratching our heads by the borders. We observe people who are stressed and hastily passing through neighborhoods and houses, devouring chocolate with apprehension. I love it like a secret recipe of concussions and a touch to the nerve of my head, with a hint of inspiration from our spices and a convenient means of cleaning off food stains. The podcast phrase highlights the actions of a culture, where leaders in various settings, including suburban areas, are causing a stir. My hair suits me perfectly, but she styles it differently according to my wishes, and this has contributed to our distinctive identities. We always want to be mindful of not overstaying our welcome, and we know that when the doors open, our time is up. It seems that we had food from Steakhouse restaurant for dinner, and we are not looking to promote unrest or chaos but to pursue peace. Although Friday the thirteenth has passed, the valley still poses challenges that require a thorough examination to avoid getting bombarded with the ubiquitous messages around us. One must take action and learn from past mistakes to prevent them from happening again.

Fridays

On Fridays we feel like we're getting closer to something better and hope that everything will turn out all right. During my lunch breaks, I usually go to the Sunshine Deli store, where I often encounter halfway emergencies, which is why some businesses operate around the clock. We agree that we should get what we deserve, a little piece of mind. All assets have terms and conditions, and statistical data is endless. Our assets have already been documented, including their specifications. The trip must be fully funded by the individual, and we acknowledge the achievements of women throughout history. Our focus is on observing the high tides, but we require two essential elements for emotional stability: sanity and devotion. Incorporating these elements in a postcard and sharing it on social media might lead to a significant positive outcome in terms of popularity. Given the tendency of people to alter their plans frequently nowadays, my decision to immediately establish a home base and subsequently travel to the opposite side of the Pacific in pursuit of uninterrupted slumber could be viewed as a countermove. Are you someone who enjoys doing multiple things simultaneously, such as sleeping, eating, and multitasking? My neighbors have a clear understanding of how to appreciate the peaceful and serene surroundings of nature. It is important to listen to them, as it rejuvenates us. Sometimes even our older neighbor Señor understands this. Although we eventually return to our own family, we have friends who stop by and engage in reasonable conversations about the nearby canyons. Comrade, Fridays tend to drag on. Hoping the weekend arrives soon so we can rest and recharge our batteries, I am looking forward to spending quality time with my loved ones and pursuing some hobbies that I haven't had the time for recently. If we were to hypothetically volunteer in Mexico City, which is 1,882 miles away and very different from Sioux City, we may face wrongful convictions, as it can happen to the innocent. With this in mind, how would we handle the situation of potentially risking an innocent person? Despite the fact that we are grateful to be alive and have a place to call home, we may not always feel happy when we return home. We prioritize the people in our lives over our own needs and constantly strive for a better future. While I hope to surprise you in the future, I prefer to keep our plans to ourselves and not make them public. We maintain a certain level of privacy and avoid unnecessary attention or interference from others.

Before we go to bed, let's make sure we are not in the path of a tornado by checking the latitudes. I need to catch a bus and buy some Fenty Beauty items for my wife, so I must prepare myself, quickly grabbing my wallet before heading out the door and making sure to double-check that I had written down the directions to the store. My mind raced with thoughts of my wife's upcoming birthday and how much I wanted to surprise her with the perfect gift. I knew that Fenty Beauty was her favorite brand, and I couldn't wait to see her excitement when I presented her with the items I had picked out. With determination in my heart and a smile on my face, I was ready to tackle the day ahead. I took a deep breath and thought about all the tasks I had to accomplish. I pulled out my notebook and reviewed my to-do list, mentally checking off each item as I went. Today was going to be a busy day, but I was determined to be productive, stay focused, and make progress toward my goals. With my headphones in and my favorite playlist playing, I knew that I was ready to tackle anything that came my way. Bring it on, I thought to myself, because today I am unstoppable. College has a remaining role in helping you get back on track, but remember that there is only so much you can fit in a can of mackerel. Instead of experimenting with electricity, like Ben Franklin, I opted for weights and dumbbells. As you review the checklist, mark off Skeeters Nursing in Rome, a fictional location. Imagine what it would have been like three hundred years ago when many items were stored on wooden ladders. As we consider the extensive effort and fortification required for constructing the Saint Pete Pier, we also acknowledge that no occupation guarantees security. Thus we opt to indulge in the delicious offerings of Haitian mangoes, five-star Haitian rum, and Borrago whiskey to unwind from the hard work. I suppose if someone's trying to find me tomorrow, I'll be on Front Street. We try to advance even in elementary school and desire a change in the weather during summer. As you mentioned, raise your shoulders and make a fist pump. In a minute we assess technology that renders robots immune to our influence. To ensure impartial decision-making, and congratulations on succeeding, I will consistently strive to have a restful night. I can't decide when I should get a physical—tomorrow or next week—so I can be on my way to better health. After a day has passed, I'm searching for job options that align with my qualifications. I plan on visiting the pool to rejuvenate so that I can't stay awake the entire night, watching baseball games, even if they are short. The key to a successful life is to surround oneself with optimistic and like-minded individuals who can guide you toward unexplored territories. Furthermore, it's crucial to continually discover new areas of expertise. We may have to venture far from our roots to spend extended periods of time in a new place, even potentially permanently, if we have the financial privilege to build a secure estate for our loved ones, which would be impressively safe. Nonetheless, we realize that we may become restless, living in such a manner. Moreover, there may be instances where a son rebels against his father. It is often an important step in a young person's development and search for personal identity. Given the limited time of the patriarch, it becomes crucial for us to emerge victorious in all situations. We need to procure it ourselves and set aside our careers. Will you rely on luck in your neighborhood? I have to fetch my child from summer camp and then go fuel up my vehicle for the concert tonight. I purchased an amazing dress for my spouse, with a considerable amount of money. I'm the individual who appeared on television before rushing to open the shop. As we move forward in life, we must continue to persevere, confront challenges, and rest. We are average individuals with creative minds who seek medical assistance for assurance of our well-being. An unidentified telegram arrived from a distant location without any indication of the owner, or perhaps it was from the World Royale. So let's venture into the town, take a brief break, and enjoy some beer. As I contemplated the potential loss of some money, I realized I couldn't dwell on it and focused on my plan to leave town. Finding a way out became my top priority at night. My plan involved spending a few hours writing, with my notes by my side, before taking a break for ginger-lemon tea. Then I would venture out to purchase more of my grandmother's home remedies. During my call with my colleague across the southern border, she mentioned her plans to return up north soon. We contemplated the possibility of finding other remote islands where we could appreciate nature in seclusion, and acknowledged that, in the desert, we must learn to live in harmony with the mosquitoes. I walked with the sooner-rather-than-later simulator in an attempt to start a new business while contemplating my next steps.

I recollected experiencing laryngitis that left me feeling off. Laryngitis is characterized by swelling in the vocal cords, which rendered me unable to speak. However, I utilized my limited sign language skills during that time. My condition was accompanied by coughing, fever, and neck pain. As it only lasted for a week and a half, it was classified as acute instead of chronic, entering my body and wishing myself luck by breaking a leg and then sending a message off to a trustworthy person so that it did not fall into the wrong hands, not being able to do things but punch a hole in the wall. I think this is worth more than words, and I leave too much pride for my own good special bulletin. As I made my way toward the distant island, I continued scanning the horizon with my binoculars. Despite being dry and sober at night, the work was still grueling, especially in the darkness. Later on I visited Seoul Market to purchase some fish for dinner but was surprised to learn that it had to be boiled. Who really boils their fish? Although emojis can bring some cheer, they aren't always enough to alleviate sadness. I strive for self-improvement, but I've learned that relying on others for help may sometimes lead to undesirable outcomes such as prolonging success or bringing bad luck.

A couple is selling ice cream cookies with two scoops on Main Street, opposite a bagel shop. They are dressed in matching uniforms and are having a great time interacting with the customers. This satisfies me, and I don't worry about losing addresses in my iPhone contacts. No one ever plans for the return trip, and I avoid disappointing or upsetting anyone. I am constantly seeking out new books to read to escape from reality and a way to expand my horizon. Occasionally we become disoriented with the changing tides rising too high. Speak softly in a subdued tone so as not to disturb those around me. My back is a little sore, and my legs are in pain. I have to acknowledge that I am aging, unless it means my birthday is approaching. During this time of year, I experience a familiar sensation in my body. It's a feeling of warmth spreading through my chest, filling me with a sense of joy and gratitude. It has been suggested to me that seeking out the most skilled animal trainer is necessary to correct a dog's behavior, and to my surprise, adding pepper to my fruit salads has greatly improved my well-being. A person's worth is determined by the dreams they have each day, and at this moment, I am completely absorbed in my aspirations for the next two days. At times we feel only partially certain about our existence. I have maintained the belief that I will not become the overweight person who is never invited to dine with others. Instead I prioritize my health and make conscious choices to maintain a balanced diet and engage in physical activity so that I can enjoy meals with friends and family without any limitations.

It's a challenging task to navigate the fear of firemen, strong winds, and brush fires in order to obtain lunar soil oxygen. I enjoy fishing for brown trout and steelheads in the Carp River, where many individuals are currently gathering worms for bait. As for my gardening plans, I intend to plant my seeds and prepare for growing blue-toned plants this year. Whenever I visit my backyard garden, I often seek advice from others who are enthusiastic to offer their suggestions. Any recommendations you might have would be greatly appreciated. Sometimes I can be a bit cautious about speaking and expressing my thoughts. Have you ever watched a film where words appear to captivate you and affect you deeply? Sometimes, when facing difficulties, you may feel vulnerable and emotional. Therefore, it's helpful to take a moment to gather yourself and remind yourself that everything will be alright. Everyone has areas of their life where they are not fully aware or conscious, such as their finances, and this is something that doesn't require an advanced degree to comprehend. Enjoy the beautiful Pocono-like landscape of Antigua, with its fields of corn, sweet potatoes, and spicy, hot chili peppers basking in the sunshine of the mountains. However, understanding engines is a prerequisite for smartness, which is a topic I am not interested in discussing. Additionally, expressing our family's emotions in public is not acceptable, as we tend to act like a pack of howling wolves. Unfortunately in this town, your voice will not be heard unless you excel in a skill that cannot be accomplished through typing. To give, you must first find a way to fit in. Despite this, in certain situations, things have a way of falling into place, like plates, forks, and knives finding their place at the dinner table. In Southwood Hills, getting a new tire may take up to three weeks, and instead of studying, the community protests. However, I enjoyed study hall and felt like part of a revolution for change. I grab food in the cafeteria and head to Greenacres, grabbing honey off the shelves and picking up Robitussin to stay alert. Be advised to take care of yourself before going to the dentist by working out from home. I enjoy salsa rice and baked potatoes as a side dish and prioritize being calm, cool, and polite. I embrace my values, positive thinking, and having friends, believing it makes up the recipe for a good life. These are the pillars that keep me grounded and help me navigate life's challenges with grace and determination. They envision a paradise with an abundance of bread and a natural flow of transactions. It's important to address problems in your community, like needing a new door. In Haitian culture, mothers are supportive from afar and are respected for their unwavering love and devotion to their children, even when they cannot physically be with them. This strong maternal bond is deeply ingrained in the Haitian community and plays a significant role in shaping the values and traditions of the culture. Whether through prayer, phone calls, or letters, Haitian mothers are always finding ways to stay connected to and encourage their children, no matter where they may be in the world. One must write a story while adorning fancy hats to gain inspiration, and connect Portuguese culture with elegant and liberal ladies, as well as orchid roses. It becomes difficult to distinguish people's thoughts due to the numerous things on their minds. Despite this, I'm passionate about research and feel that we can convince ourselves that we deserve a Nobel Peace Prize.

I am determined to maintain my subscriptions and encourage others to join. There is a graveyard shift in fifty-eight days—tell them to come on in. Hopefully your car won't break down due to unforeseen issues while I go to the Madison River to make some money. Sometimes helping others is all it takes. I will fight, and then we'll let it blow over; it's our method of handling it. Understanding changes in war; plans and reservations are crucial and offer hope for a more peaceful future. By learning from past conflicts, analyzing current situations and anticipating future scenarios, we can make informed decisions and take proactive measures to prevent and mitigate the devastating consequences of war. This requires not only the involvement of governments and military leaders, but also of civil society, academia, and international organizations, who can provide different perspectives, expertise, and resources to enhance our collective effort towards building a safer and more just world. Ultimately, understanding changes in war can help us prioritize diplomacy, dialogue, and cooperation over aggression, violence, and division, and create a culture of peace that values human life, dignity, and diversity above all. I have enough to stay awake, though I'm exhausted. By the end of the week, I'll feel like I've aged twenty years. Work smarter, not harder, and we'll prepare for tonight's party. Never decline an opportunity—let's be quick. Your phone might be low on charge, and your dog may turn on you, but you'll still enter a store only to find it's half-price. Keep practicing your swings even if it means dealing with gophers in your garden. Let's go to Frank Pepe's Pizzeria, hear some stories, and think about how many words we know. As we sit down with our delicious Neapolitan pizza, we start discussing the origins of certain words and find ourselves expanding our vocabulary with each passing moment. Despite being busy with chores and gatherings in the home, we must operate efficiently. Leopards climb trees for food, babies get sick, and decorations are essential at this time of year. We'll head to the living room; not sure when exactly it'll be, but we'll still be excited. Legislation seems to have found a way to overcome blackmailing tactics. I have an incredible vision of a spacious house with a beautiful view, complete with a small concession that has us all excited. I need to be ready for anything and always have good news on hand while watching *Blue Bloods* and promoting our fast 10G network and offerings. We enjoy cuisine from all corners of the world, but not everyone can afford caviar. As we age, we become more careful since our recovery rate is not what it used to be, and certain things become impossible. Thankfully we have great friends who understand us. Rather than engage in risky behavior like drinking and driving, we should focus on being better at public relations. We must communicate clearly to maintain healthy relationships and avoid misunderstandings. Redeeming ourselves can be challenging, but as long as we maintain our nerves and stay composed, we can overcome any obstacle. We must keep our priorities straight and focus on business, even when we meet attractive people. Moving into a respectable environment, going to Café Road, and having the occasional good day are all essential elements of a fulfilling life. Be cautious when heading up to Sunrise, and watch out for evil spirits that may communicate messages. When surveying unclaimed land, pay attention to the birds that fly above and document important details. Talk to the judge to ensure you pay what you owe. Capitalize on any opportunities and become a real estate investor. Wait for calls back, continue working on projects, and try to avoid jaywalking tickets. Inject some jazz fever into your life and enjoy the ride!

Due to our hunger, we have decided to dine at the diner and order a side of house salad. The weather is beautiful, and before dessert, we plan to enjoy some boring pizza while I am still wearing my overalls. Feeling burnt out from the previous day, I head to the local supply house for some home goods. Looking back on the past, party nights were smoother, and the games we played were different, but now we have to work, even on our days off. It's okay if you're not familiar with America's sixteenth president or the famous Gettysburg Address. Sometimes we watch videos on how to relax and enjoy our days, but we still have to do household chores like dishes while singing a melody. Although I don't like getting sick, it happens, and rest is crucial. I plan to make lentil soup from the bottom of the oven. If I have time, I will figure out what's going on downstairs and have someone help me. If you have nothing to do, gambling in the afternoon may not be a bad idea, as it could rake in hundreds or thousands of dollars. Some people influence us to visit Broadway, so we dress up nicely and select something marvelous to wear. Sometimes letters get misplaced, and people can be highly emotional. We treat ourselves to the beautiful National Harbor waterfront resort and have secret weapons in our kitchen for our cuisines. When we were younger, we had to learn the value of money on our own because no one else would teach us. In a few days, we plan to go where we can remember good old memories. By echoing our voice, we can find the way out, and we still need to check for updates. Before heading to work, I think about what to say to impress others during Mardi Gras and don't have time to rely on others' help. If I need something done, I must do it myself at Fairchild's Wheeler, where we hit golf balls and constantly think of new designs to complement the ones we already have. Before going to the office, we organize everything in the garage, and advertising thoughts bubble in our heads. We don't regret anything we do, because everything we do has been brilliant. We're always prepared to start a business, and we hope to come up with magnificent ideas that will be recognized by others. We boil potatoes, fry eggs, and decide to eat in rather than dine at a restaurant. Later I'll make a decisive choice. People's minds are essential to everything, and we want to help honest people who deserve it. We plan to post regularly on social media to ensure everything goes according to plan. We should never take anyone for granted, and it's important to change the subject when things get heated. Life is unpredictable, and we must spend time doing things we love, whether it's spending time with our car or drawing dogs. We must remain civilized and work hard to stay out of trouble. Supporting locally owned businesses is vital, and we're willing to pay seventy-five dollars or less for trendy items. Some prefer to visit upscale places like the Buckhead Butcher Shop for an apparent accommodation. It's important to keep the lucky streak going and not lose too much money. I'll head up to the hills to purchase some bricks I've been meaning to buy for a while. After the tools have been delivered, we'll get to work patching things up and hire some labor workers for extra help. Working without pay isn't right, and we take regular breaks for 16:8 intermittent fasting, drinking water, and getting a manicure. It is important to prioritize self-care and rest to maintain a healthy work-life balance and avoid burnout. Marriage requires effort, sensitivity, and understanding, but we must also apologize when necessary. We strive to make no obscenities and to help those who deserve it. Anything is possible, and we ensure everything is running smoothly. We must be able to sleep at night, and we should never let differences ruin our friendships. We receive social invitations, and politicians must react to people's needs and concerns in order to effectively represent their constituents and serve the community. It's essential to vote, have a busy itinerary, and accomplish official tasks before indulging in unofficial ones. I have gray hair and old sneakers from high school, but the chicks still think I'm cool. Maybe it's my laid-back attitude, or my taste in music or the stories I tell, but whatever it is, I'm just glad the ladies still find me charming. As kids we did foolish things like throwing eggs at passing cars and breaking streetlights. Still, now I must update my license at the motor vehicle office before it expires or else I won't be able to drive legally and could face penalties if caught. I know the lines at the motor vehicle office are long and tedious, but I have no other option but to make time for this task. It's only a small inconvenience compared to the consequences of driving without a valid license. Plus, having a valid license gives me the freedom to go wherever I want and do whatever I need to do. So, I'll just have to suck it up, gather my documents, and head to the motor vehicle office before it's too late. I hurry to North Shore Super Groceries and support our military by purchasing care package items to send to deployed troops overseas. Heights don't scare us since writing without looking has made us courageous. We've learned to face our fears with confidence, knowing that we can accomplish anything with practice and determination. While shopping for cheap hardware with others who know nothing about electricity or fixing faded walls, I always say that I must strike while the iron is hot, otherwise I might miss out on a great opportunity. It's important to take action when the timing is right, whether it's pursuing a new job, investing in a stock, or making a big life change. Waiting too long or hesitating can often lead to regret or missed chances. So when I feel that sense of inspiration or motivation, I try to act on it quickly and decisively, knowing that the window of opportunity may not stay open for long. Effective meetings are crucial, and refined crude oil lubricates my engine. We volunteer for Habitat for Humanity and represent great work with integrity and support worthy causes that make a positive impact in the lives of individuals and communities. Our dedication to service goes beyond just building homes, as we believe in creating a sustainable future for those in need. Through our efforts, we hope to inspire others to join us in making a difference and promoting a better world for all. Everything has a price, which is time and effort. The value we place on these things is reflected in the allocation of our time and the degree of effort we are willing to expend. In the end the price we pay in time and effort determines the significance and true worth of the things we hold most dear. Therefore, termites destroy things, and we must always be vigilant to prevent them from causing irreparable damage to our homes and properties.

Starting with various ideas results in a lot of hypocrisy. The pressure from large corporations can be intense, and one needs to understand how it feels to be offered a few services. However, it provides us with the freedom to express ourselves openly. Let's walk to Chipotle and savor their delicious sofritas dish. It may not be the best day to eat out, but we can still enjoy our meal, with mothers being mothers and newborns picking joyful careers. Progress is essential, but we should still stick to our plan of having our child attend med school and receive fantastic gifts. Despite being from different parts of the world, we are all interconnected through media technologies. I cannot discriminate and resist salary issues; a short photography session will satisfy my desire to capture beautiful moments and memories with my camera. It's better to claim a bad situation than to create false value for earning royalty money. Having a great sense of humor is crucial in life, and we must learn to laugh at our mistakes. Our daily decisions profoundly impact our lives, and we should act ethically. Good gestures are an excellent way to compliment someone, and we should stick to them. We need to look beyond detours and distractions in life and keep moving forward. The path to success is not always linear, and detours and distractions are just a part of the journey. We should remember that the family owns the property investment that loves music and solitude; they don't like being disturbed. We are having to take our nerve medicines to stay calm and enjoy our peanut-butter-with-cream-cheese-and-jelly sandwich with some orange juice. As we savor each bite, we feel the anxiety and stress of the day melt away, leaving us with a moment of pure pleasure and contentment. The richness and depth of flavors awaken our senses and transport us to a place of blissful indulgence. With each mouthful, we are reminded of the simple joys in life that we sometimes overlook in our busy lives. As we relish in the moment, we are grateful for the time to slow down and enjoy the food and company around us. The weatherman predicts rain tomorrow, adding to the list of burned-out stoves and blurred images that we have encountered. It's like being a fighter in the ring—there's a lot of viciousness, including the silhouette of Tyson Fury. Nonetheless, there is still ample room for us to work and improve. We need confirmation to move forward and would be thrilled if you would join us. While a positive outcome would be preferable, let's remain open to life's path and keep embracing what we tell ourselves.